This Book Belongs To

Copyright © Greg Smith 2024
All rights reserved. This book or any part thereof may not be used without written consent from the author or illustrator.

Author and Aboriginal art: Greg Smith
Illustrator and book design: Leila Warne

I.S.B.N:
Published by Yama 2 You Bush tucker nursery.
yama2youbooks@outlook.com

G'day Folks! My name is Greg from Yama2You Bush Tucker Nursery. This book is designed to teach all Australians how to connect with and care for Country. We can connect to Country by choosing our favourite native plant or animal. Caring for country is to learn all that you can about your plant or animal and learn how to look after and protect it.

I'm so excited that you are about to learn about some of our very special Australian plants, but please remember the number one rule, NEVER EVER eat anything from the bush without permission from an adult or Elder.

Lemon Myrtle

Backhousia Citriodora
Size: 6m - 20m
Flowers: creamy/white in spring - summer
Fruits: mid to late autumn/early spring
Harvest: all year round, the smaller leaves are best

Traditional Use

The leaves are used to make tea or for inhaling the steam for colds and flu. The leaves can be crushed and made into a paste to treat wounds. The lemon myrtle leaves are also used to add flavour to food.

Lemon Myrtle attracts bees, birds, butterflies, cockatoos, Blue-faced Honeyeaters, Lewin's honey eaters and nectar eating birds.

Modern Use

Tea, cooking and essential oils

Tastes Like:

Sherbet lemon

Lemon Myrtle - Blue banded bee - Blue-faced Honeyeater

Old Man Saltbush

Atriplex nummularia

Size: 3 meters tall and up to 5 meters wide.
Flowers and fruits: Small cream/pink flowers and bright pink/red berries throughout the year.

Traditional Use
The Saltbush fruits were eaten and provided Vitamin C. The seeds were used in damper. The leaves were used to flavour meat and the grubs living on the leaves and roots were eaten for protein.

Old Man Saltbush attracts: Parrots, finches, goannas, lizards, and insects. Butterflies lay their eggs on the foliage.

Modern Use
Today, Saltbush is used in cooking. It's a great salt replacement with 20% less sodium than table salt. Saltbush is used in farming to reduce salt levels in soil and for cattle to eat.

Tastes Like:
Salty leaf with earthy undertones.

Old Man Saltbush - Small Eastern Spinebill

Tasmanian Mountain Pepper

Tasmannia Lanceolata
Size: 2-10 meters tall
Flowers: Male and female cream coloured flowers in summer
Fruits: small dark berries in autumn

Traditional Use
Tasmanian Mountain Pepper was used for flavouring, preservation and for medicinal purposes. It has antibacterial properties and was used as a tea.

Tasmanian Mountain Pepper attracts birds such as the Yellow Throated Honeyeater or the Dusk Robin, bees and other insects.

Modern Use
The berries and/or leaves are used to flavour food or as a seasoning.

Tastes like:
A berry flavour with peppery heat

Tasmanian Mountain Pepper - Tasmanian devil - Yellow Shouldered Bee - Common Brown Butterfly

Warrigal Greens

Tetragonia tetragonioides
Size: 50cm tall
Flowers: small yellow flowers.
Harvest: throughout the year.

Modern Use
Historically, Warrigal Greens were one of the first foods eaten by Captain Cook's crew to ward off scurvy. Today it is used as a spinach as it is high in fiber, vitamins and antioxidants. Warrigal greens can be eaten raw in salads but only in small amounts but is better blanched or cooked as it cooks out the oxalates.

Warrigal Greens attract lizards, snails, caterpillars, moths, and ladybirds. Warrigal Greens make great ground cover in a garden.

Traditional Use

Warrigal Greens were rarely eaten by First Nations People.

Tastes Like:
Spinach

Warrigal Greens - native ladybirds - native brown snails

Quondong

Santalum acuminatum
Size: 2-7 meters tall.
Flowers: small, cream, cup shaped flowers in late summer.
Harvest: bright red, waxy fruit the following spring.

Traditional Use

The fruit and nuts were a great source of food.
The leaves were crushed and mixed with saliva to treat skin sores and the wood was used to make bowls and coolamons.

Quondongs attract insects, birds and emus.

Didge ya know that Quondong seeds need emus and other animals to eat them and poop them out to help them germinate?

Modern Use

The Quondong seeds are used for essential oils or eating. The fruit is eaten fresh, juiced, made into jam, cordial, pies or tea.

Tastes Like:

Sour peach/citrus and they contain twice the amount of vitamin C than an orange.

Quondong - Emu

Kangaroo Grass

Themeda triandra
Size: 1.5 meters tall.
Flowers: October - March
Harvest: late December, when the seeds turn a dark brown.

Traditional Use

The dried Grass was used to start fires and the seeds were ground into a flour to make damper or Johnny cakes.

Kangaroo Grass attracts birds, emus, wombats, kangaroos, wallabies and butterflies.

Modern Use

Kangaroo Grass is now being farmed and milled into flour that is naturally gluten free.

Kangaroo Grass - Wombat - Eastern Ground Parrot - Southern Dart Butterfly

Finger Lime

Citrus australasica
Size: 2 - 7 meters tall.
Flowers: White and pink flowers in June.
Harvest: December - May.

The thorny Finger lime shrubs/trees attract butterflies, bees, wasps, ants and birds.

Traditional Use

Finger limes were eaten straight off the tree and used to flavour food (such as meat or fish). Finger limes are high in vitamin C and were often used to prevent cold and flu.

Modern Use

Finger limes are used fresh in salads, desserts or as a garnish or to flavour cordials, jams, and jellies.

Tastes Like:

citrus/lime

Finger Lime - Blue triangle Butterfly

Yam Daisy

Murnong - *Microseris lanceolata*
Size: 30cm tall.
Flowers: Yellow flowers, Spring - Autumn
Harvest: the leaves and flowers are harvested between spring and autumn. Tubers are harvested after flowering.

Yam Daisies attract bees, insects, birds, butterflies and tuber loving animals such as a bandicoot.

Traditional Use

Yam Daisies were a stable food source. The leaves were eaten raw or cooked and the tubers were roasted on coals.
The tubers are high in carbohydrates

Modern Use

The flowers are used in salads or an edible decoration. The tubers are roasted and eaten. The flowers and leaves can also be used for dyeing fabrics.

Tastes Like:

Tubers taste like sweet potato.

Yam Daisy - Bandicoot - Hoverfly

Bush Tomato

Solanum Central

Size: 30 - 45 cm tall.
Flowers: mauve/purple flowers late summer to spring.
Harvest: in autumn and winter once the fruit has dried on the shrub.

Bush Tomato (desert raisin) plants attract birds, bees, butterflies, bush turkeys, emus and mice.

Traditional Use

Bush tomatoes were eaten straight off the plant (once dried out) as a source of food and to flavour meat. They were also a source of bush medicine.

Modern Use

Used to flavour food such as damper, salsa, sauces and chutneys. Bush Tomato can be added to stock to increase depth of flavour.

Tastes Like:

caramelised tomato or a tomarillo.

Bush Tomato - Hopping mouse

Lomandra

Lomandra Longifolia
Size: 60 - 80 cm tall.
Flowers: small cream flowers early spring.
Harvest: Collect seeds February to April.

Lomandra attracts snakes, lizards, bees, ants, beetles and butterflies.

Traditional Use

Lomandra leaves, also known as mat rush, were used for weaving nets, baskets, dilly bags, fishing nets/baskets and mats.
The seeds were dried, crushed and milled into a flour.
The base of its leaves was chewed for food and water.

Modern Use
The seeds are milled and ground into flour.
The flowers are edible and taste like peas.

Tastes Like:
seeds taste like a nutty grain and the base of the leaves taste like celery.

Lomandra - Blue Tongued Lizard - Zebra Finches

Davidson Plum

Davidsonia jerseyana
Size: 5 - 12 meters tall.
Flowers: small dark pink flowers November - February.
Harvest: February - May.

Traditional Use

Davidson plums were a food source and a preservative for meat.
The trunks of the trees were used to make tools and weapons such as harpoons for hunting turtles.

Davidson Plums attracts insects, birds, bees, tree kangaroos, king parrots and possums.

Modern Use

Deserts, sauces, jams, jellies cordials, vinaigrettes and chocolate.

Tastes Like:
Sour plum

Davidson plum - Tree Kangaroo

Wattle

Acacia longifolia

Size: 3 - 10 Meters.
Flowers: early winter to spring.
Harvest: green pods can be harvested in Spring. The seeds are then harvested late spring-summer.

Traditional Use

The wattle flowers can be steeped in water for tea or used to make a yellow dye.
The bark has antiseptic properties and also used as a dye.
The leaves were ground with water to make a soap or to use for fishing.
The sap was used as a cold/flu remedy, as a resin or glue.
The timber was used to make tools and the seeds were ground to make flour

Wattle attracts birds (e.g. the little wattle bird), bees, butterflies, ants and other insects.
Cockatoos strip the bark looking for insects to eat.

Modern Use

Now used in cooking as flour, can be used as a coffee substitute. Added to damper, biscuits or scones.

Tastes like:

Nutty coffee/chocolate flavours.

Wattle - King Parrot

She Oak

Casuarina
Size: 3 - 20 meters
Fruits: young green nut/cone.
December - February

She Oaks attract Cockatoos (e.g. Red-tailed black cockatoo, Yellow tailed black cockatoo, Gang gang cockatoo) and Galahs.

Didge ya know?
The Glossy Black Cockatoo only eats the seeds off the She Oaks, because of land clearing; the Glossy Black Cockatoos are now endangered.

Traditional Use

The young green nuts were eaten fresh or cooked. Chewing the nuts or foliage helped with thirst.
The wood of the She Oak was used to make shelters, tools and firewood.

All over Australia

Modern Use
Recently the green nuts have been used in jams or tea.

Tastes like:
Woody green apple

She Oak - Yellow Tailed Black Cockatoo

Native Ginger

Alpinia caerulea
Size: 2 meters.
Flowers: White flowers in spring
Fruits: Bright blue berries in summer
Harvest: Berries in summer, leaves and tubers all year round .

Native ginger attracts birds (e.g. Red-headed Honeyeaters), bees, butterflies and other insects.

Traditional Use

The leaves were used to line the roof of a humpy.
The berries, leaves, shoots, roots and tubers were all eaten. The leaves often being wrapped around food before cooking to enhance the flavour.

Modern Use

Native Ginger is now used as an indoor/outdoor plant and is used in cooking, tea and the berries are eaten fresh.

Tastes like:

Mild ginger. Berries taste like fruit salad.

Native Ginger - Red-headed Honeyeater - Blue Banded Bee - Banded Demon Butterfly

Lillypilly

Syzygium smithii
Size: up to 20 meters tall.
Flowers: October - March.
Harvest: winter fruiting. May - August.

Lillypilly attracts possums, bees, butterflies, birds (e.g. Bower birds, native pigeons, fruit doves, parrots) and flying foxes.
Lillypilly provides shelter and nesting sites.

Traditional Use

The Lillypilly berries were eaten fresh or dried and stored to eat later. They were a great source of vitamin C.

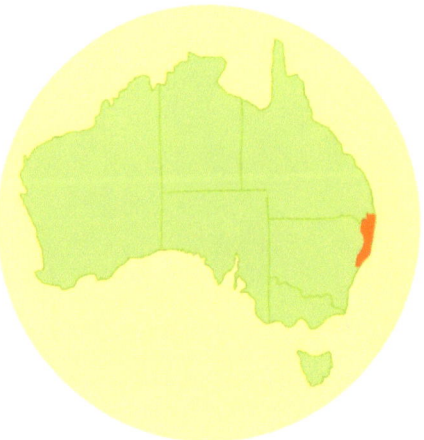

Modern Use

Cordial, jam, chutney, muffins, cakes, pies, wine and skin care products

Tastes like:

Clove, apple and spiced berry

Lilly Pilly - Sugar Gliders

Pigface

Carpobrotus
Size: 10 cm tall but will spread as a ground cover.
Flower: Bright Pink daisy like flowers.
Spring - Summer.
Fruits: Red fruit in summer

Pigface attracts ants, moths, butterflies, bees, kangaroos, wombats, wallabies and possums.

Traditional Use

The Pigface fruit was eaten fresh or dried.
The leaves were eaten fresh or used to soother sun burn, burns, stings or mixed with water and gargles to ease sore throats.

Modern Use

cooking, jams and pickles.

Tastes like:

The leaves taste like aloe vera or cucumber. The fruit tastes like a salty kiwi fruit.

Pigface - Brush tailed possum - Cressida Cressida Butterfly

Peppermint Gum

Eucalyptus Dives
Size: Up to 20 meters.
Flowers: white flowers, Spring - Summer.
Harvest: The leaves are able to be harvested all year round.

Traditional Use
The roots were tapped for water when needed.
The leaves were used to treat cold and flu through steam inhalation or tea.

Peppermint Gum attracts birds, bees, koalas, and provides food and habitat.

Modern Use
Essential oil, tea, cakes, chocolates, cough lollies,

Tastes Like:
Peppermint and Eucalyptus

Peppermint Gum - Koala

Wattle Seed Damper

Ingredients

3 Cups of self raising flour
100 gm butter, cubed
2 tablespoons ground wattle seed + extra for on top.

Method

Put the flour in a large mixing bowl and add the cubed butter. Squish the butter and flour with your fingers until you have a bread crumb like consistency. Add the 2 tablespoons of wattle seed and the milk. Stir with a fork or knead into a dough. Fold into a ball, score the top and add sprinkle the leftover wattle seed on top. Bake in a re heated oven 180C for 20-25 minutes until golden brown and hollow sounding when you tap the top.

Ingredients

250 gm butter
250 gm sugar
1 tsp vanilla paste
1 1/2 tsp lemon myrtle powder
3 cup of plain flour
1/2 tsp baking powder

Method

Put butter and sugar in a mixer and mix on medium speed. Add the vanilla, lemon myrtle powder, flour and baking powder and mix until you have a bread crumb like consistency. Remove the bowl from the mixer and knead the mixture together with your hands, adding the milk to help bring it all together. Roll a tablespoon of the dough in your hands, flatten between your palms and place on a (greased or lined) baking sheet.
Bake in a preheated oven (180C) for 10 minutes.

Kangaroo Stew

serves 6

Ingredients:

1 kg kangaroo steak cut into cubes
4 tbs of ground bush tomato
1 tbs mountain pepper
3 pinches of salt
1 1/2 cups of gravy
1 can tinned tomatoes
2 onions, diced
2 cloves garlic
5 small potatoes, cubed
3 sticks celery, chopped
2 carrots, chopped
2 spring onions, chopped

Method:

Add all the ingredients to the pot.

Stove top - bring to the boil and then simmer, with the lid on, for 2 hours.
Slow cooker - minimum 4 hours
Insta cooker/pressure cooker - stew setting or 35 minutes.

Lemon Myrtle Tea

Steep 3-4 fresh lemon myrtle
leaves or 1/2 teaspoon
dried leaves
in freshly boiled water
for 2 minutes
or longer if you like strong
tea. Strain into a cup and
add sugar if you like
it sweetened.

Davidson Plum Cordial

Ingredients:
3 tbs Davidson plum powder
1 cup caster sugar
1 cup water
1/2 tsp citric acid

Method
In a pot, bring the sugar and water to the boil. Once the sugar is dissolved take the pot off the heat and carefully add the Davidson plum powder and citric acid. Stir the powder in and the bring back to the boil. Allow to bubble for 2 minutes. Remove from the heat and allow to cool. Strain the syrup into a clean jar or bottle.
To use, add to glass and add water. Makes 2-3 litres depending on taste.

About the author

Greg Smith is an Aboriginal man whose grandmother was from the stolen generation. His grandmother knew very little of her culture or history which is what has inspired Greg to learn and teach. Greg's passion is sharing the knowledge he has gained with the coming generations and believes that the future lies in love, passion and knowledge of Country.

Follow Greg's journey on his Instagram page
instagram.com/Yama2you

With special thanks to all the aunties, uncles, schools and companies that have helped along the way. We are truly grateful for your encouragement, help and wisdom.

www.ingramcontent.com/pod-product-compliance
Lightning Source LLC
Chambersburg PA
CBHW041708160426
43209CB00017B/1776